I0467773

Stoney Creek Ontario in Colour Photos, Saving Our History One Photo at a Time

Photography
by Barbara Raué
2014

Series Name:
Cruising Ontario

Book 62: Stoney Creek in Colour

Cover photo: Battlefield House taken from Stoney Creek Battlefield Monument

Series Name: Cruising Ontario
Saving Our History One Photo at a Time

Check the Appendixes in the back of each book for
descriptions of architectural terms and building styles

Other Books by Barbara Raue

Coins of Gold

Arrows, Indians and Love

The Life and Times of Barbara
Volume 1: Inventions That Have Enhanced My Life
Volume 2: Entertainment That I Have Enjoyed
Volume 3: East Coast Trips
Volume 4: Olympics Have Always Intrigued Me
Volume 5: Wonders of the World
Volume 6: Caribbean Cruises We Have Enjoyed
Volume 7: Animals
Volume 8: Storms and Other Major Disasters in My Lifetime
Volume 9: Wars, Terrorist Attacks and Major Disasters

The Cromwell Family Book

Stoney Creek

Stoney Creek is located on the south-western shore of Lake Ontario into which feed the watercourse of Stoney Creek as well as several other minor streams. It was settled by Loyalists after the American Revolution. The Battle of Stoney Creek during the War of 1812 occurred near Centennial Parkway and King Street. In a surprise night-time attack, the outnumbered British overwhelmed the Americans and forced their retreat to Forty Mile Creek (the present location of Grimsby). In this forty minute battle, hundreds were killed and the two American Generals were captured. Battlefield Park has a monument and museum to preserve the history of this area.

Branches of the Bruce Trail provide access to Battlefield Park as well as the Devil's Punch Bowl which is marked by a large illuminated cross and offers an excellent lookout for Stoney Creek and Hamilton.

The Stoney Creek Dairy on King Street, with a stylized Battlefield Monument in its logo, offered frozen treats for decades. In 2013, the dairy was torn down for re-development. Eastgate Square Mall straddles the former border between Hamilton and Stoney Creek.

Due to the temperate environment, the Stoney Creek area is known for fruit growing. Most of the land mass of Stoney Creek remains agricultural. The communities of Elfrida, Fruitland, Tapleytown, Tweedside, Vinemount, and Winona are agricultural areas.

Stoney Creek became a centre for light industry, road transportation and commuting residences, since its land costs were much lower than in neighbouring Hamilton.

E.D. Smith was established in 1878 in the Niagara Peninsula when a young farmer experimented with grapes, onions, hens, cows, sheep, grain, and a little patch of strawberries. The place was 120 acres tucked under the protective shadow of the Escarpment in Ontario's Niagara Peninsula. He hoped to make a living by harvesting the strawberries and taking the fruit to market. The juicy strawberries that grew so well in this rich soil were the beginning of a food empire. Its current product line includes jams and spreads, syrups, pie fillings, ketchup, sauces, and salad dressings.

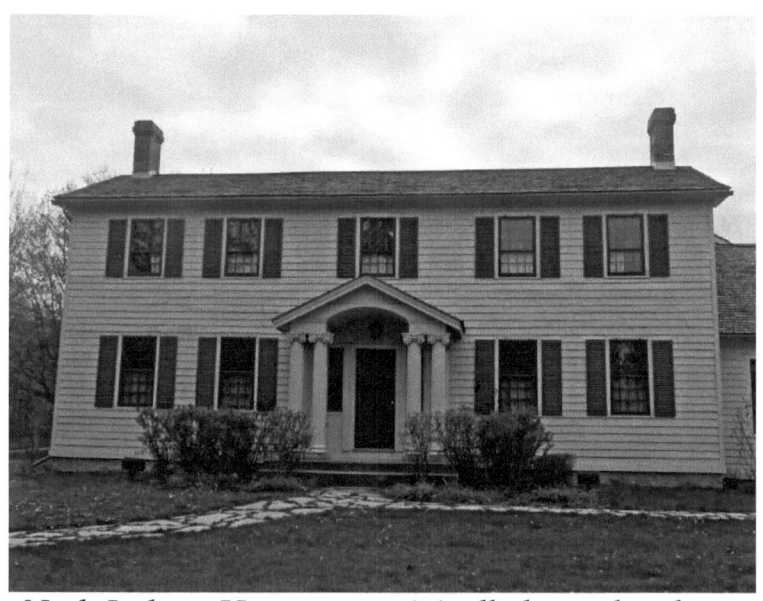

The Nash-Jackson House was originally located at the north-east corner of King Street East and Nash Road in Hamilton. The house was built in 1818 in the Georgian style. The house was moved to Stoney Creek Battlefield Park in 1999.

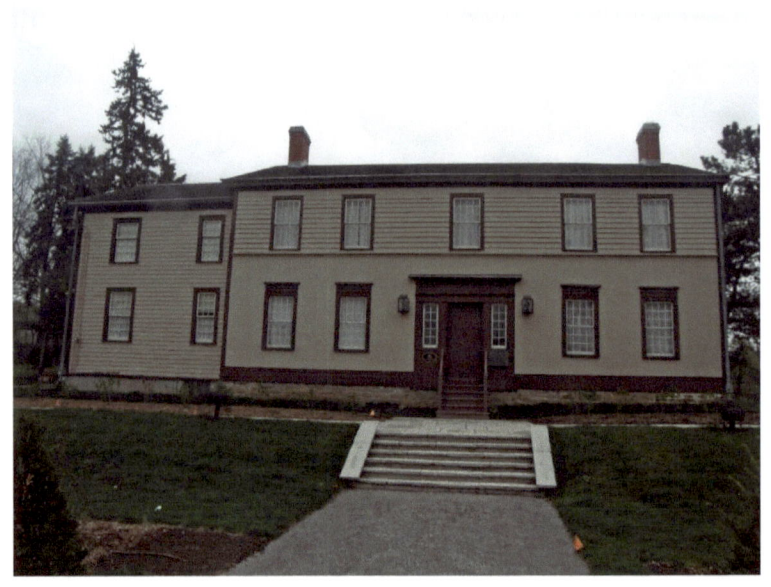

Battlefield House, 77 King Street West, circa 1796,
Georgian style

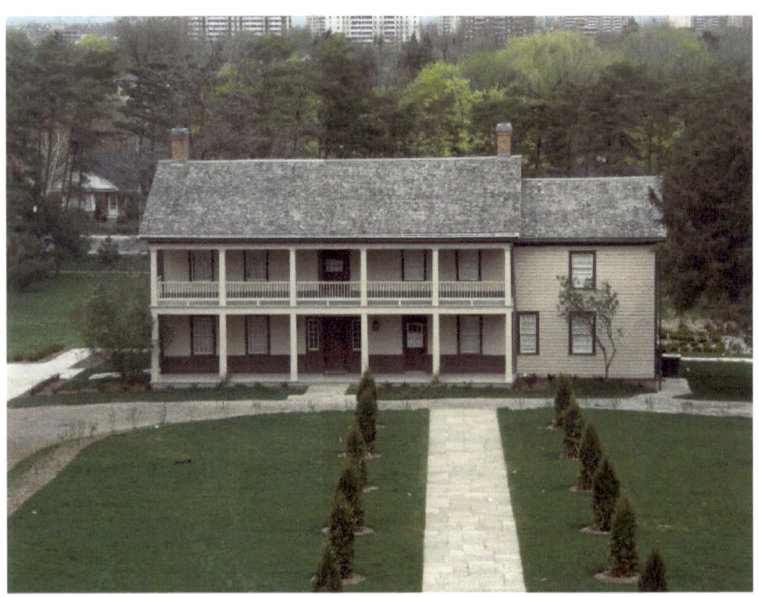

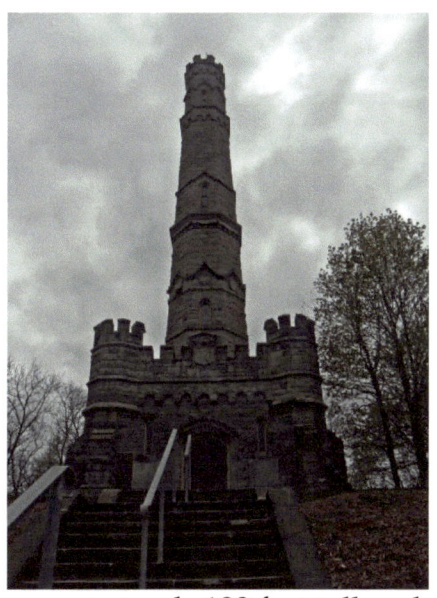

Battlefield Monument stands 100 feet tall and commemorates a century of peace between the British and the Americans.

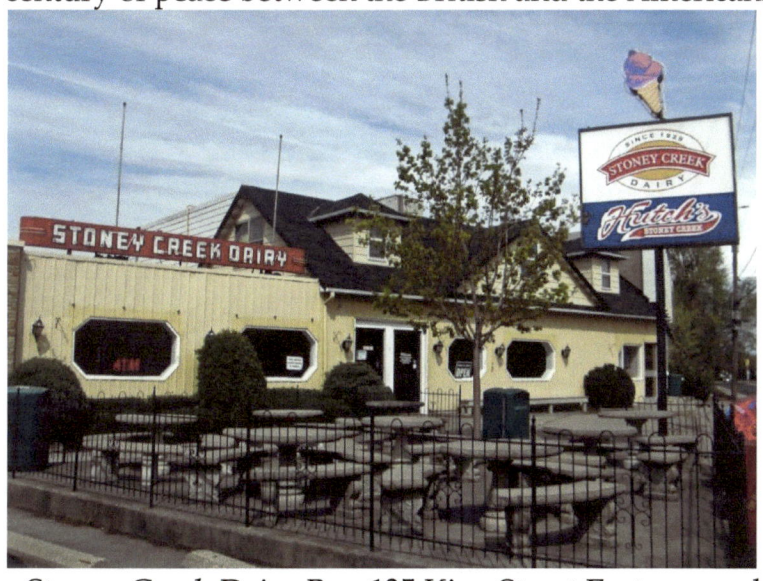

The Stoney Creek Dairy Bar, 135 King Street East, opened in 1941 to serve frozen treats. It closed in 2012.

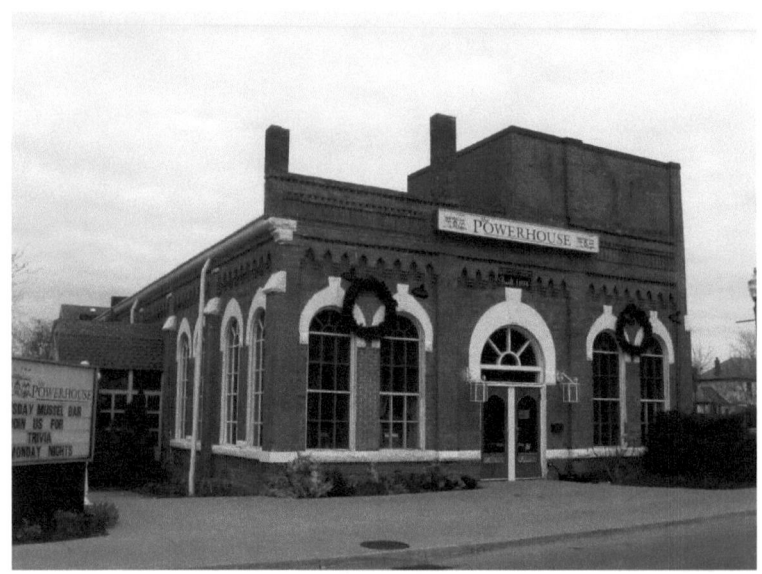

The Powerhouse is a historical landmark at the centre of Stoney Creek, 21 Jones Street. It provided power for electric rail lines in the 1890s. Now it is a restaurant.

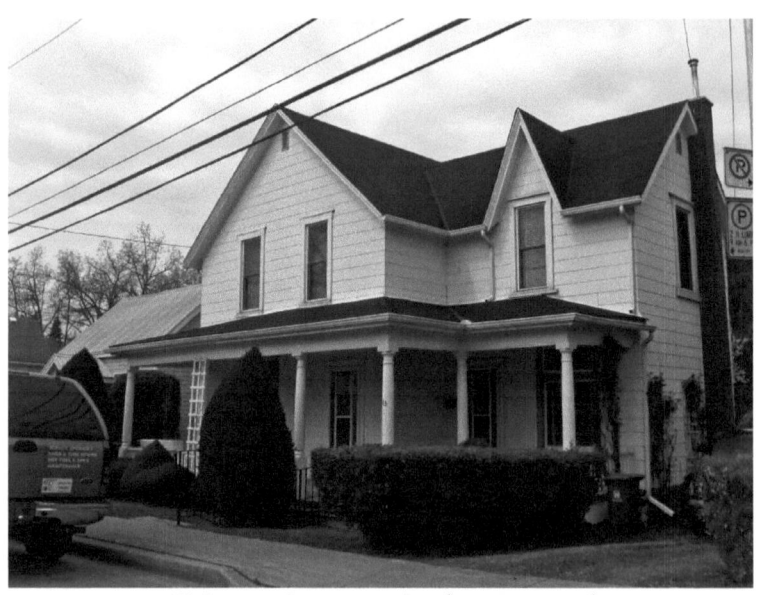

15 Jones Street – Gothic Revival

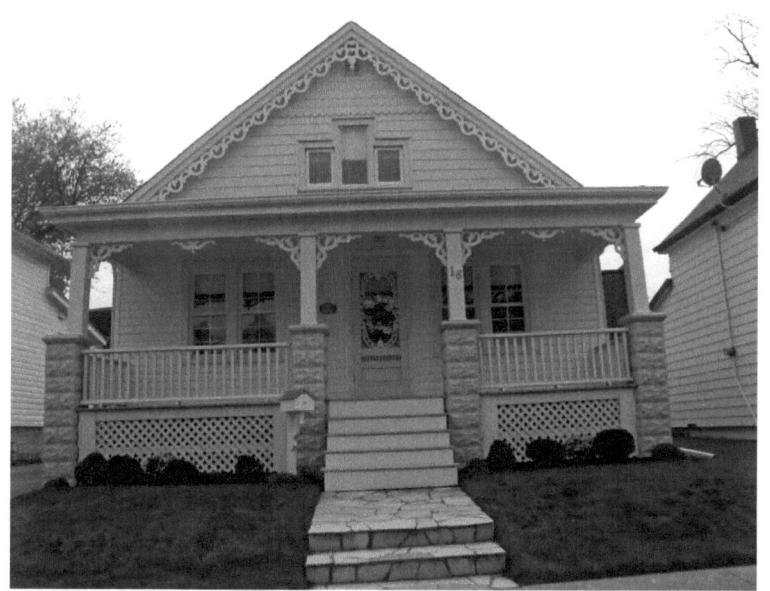

16 Jones Street – Gothic Revival, vergeboard trim on gable, Palladian window

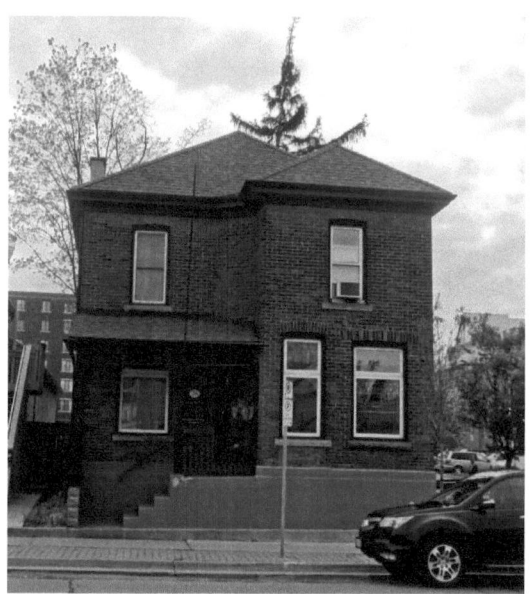

26 King Street – Italianate, hip roof

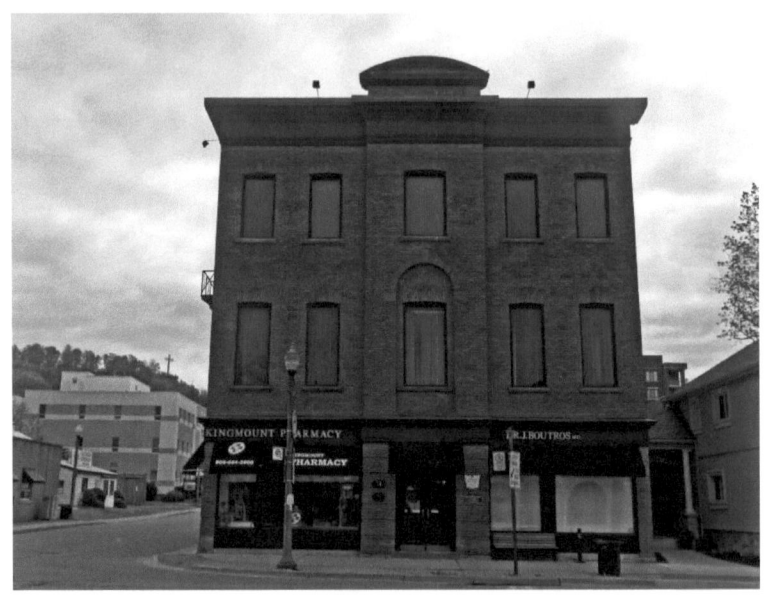

Century Square - 1901

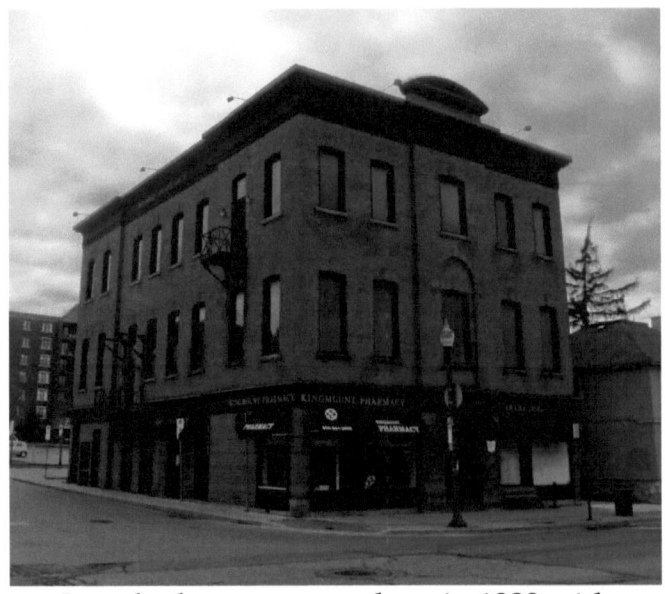

I worked a co-op term here in 1989 with
Architect Jerry Herringa.

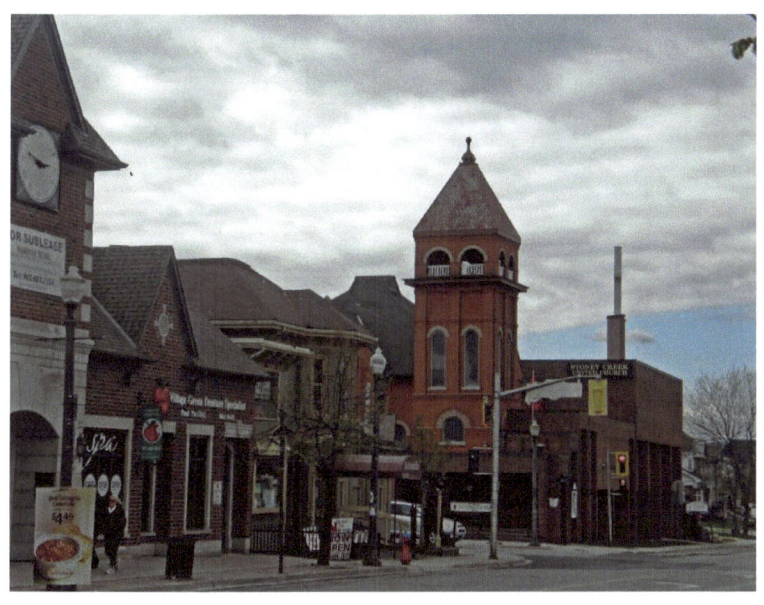

Downtown Stoney Creek

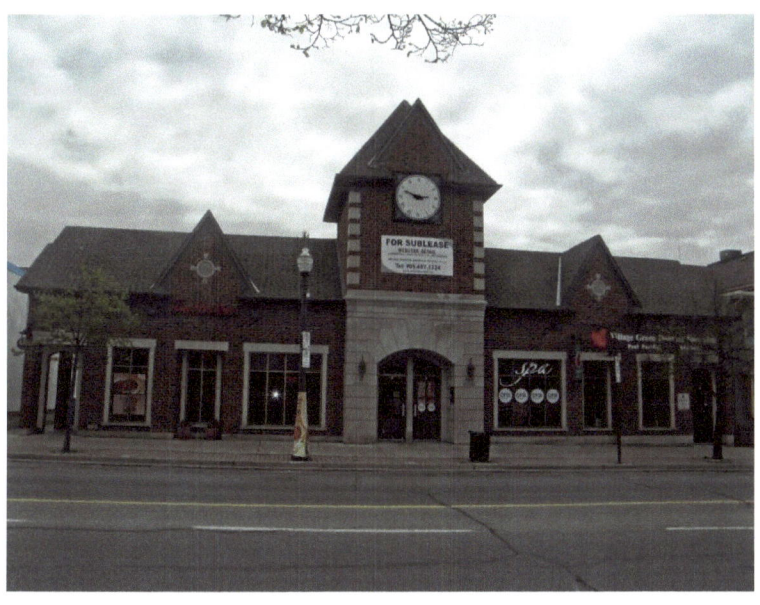

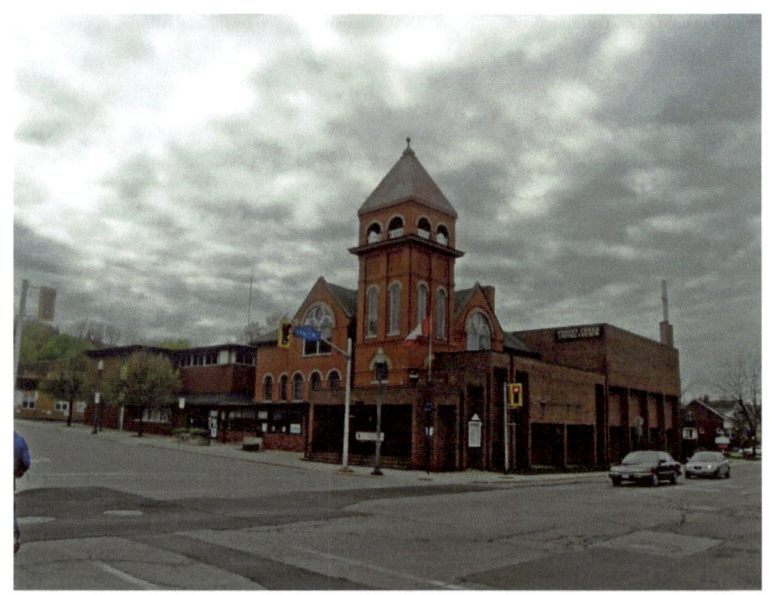

Stoney Creek United Church, 1 King Street, corner of Lake
Avenue, founded in 1792

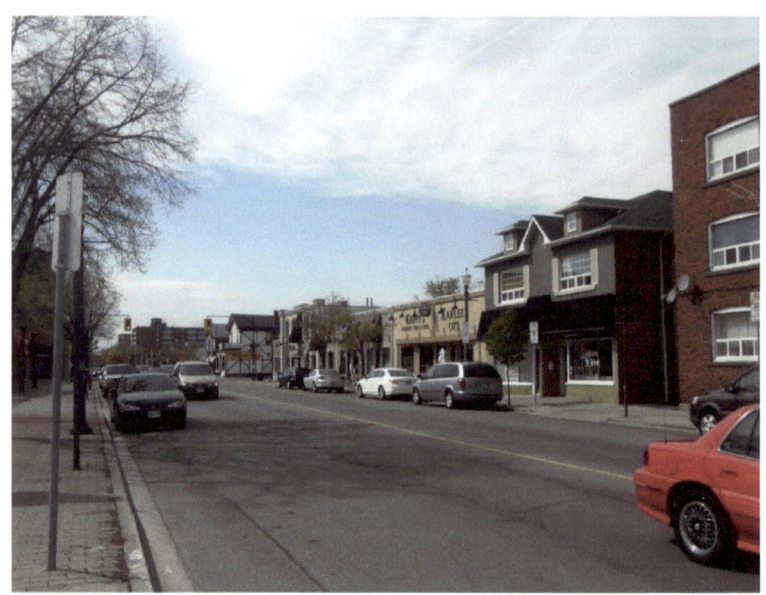

King Street

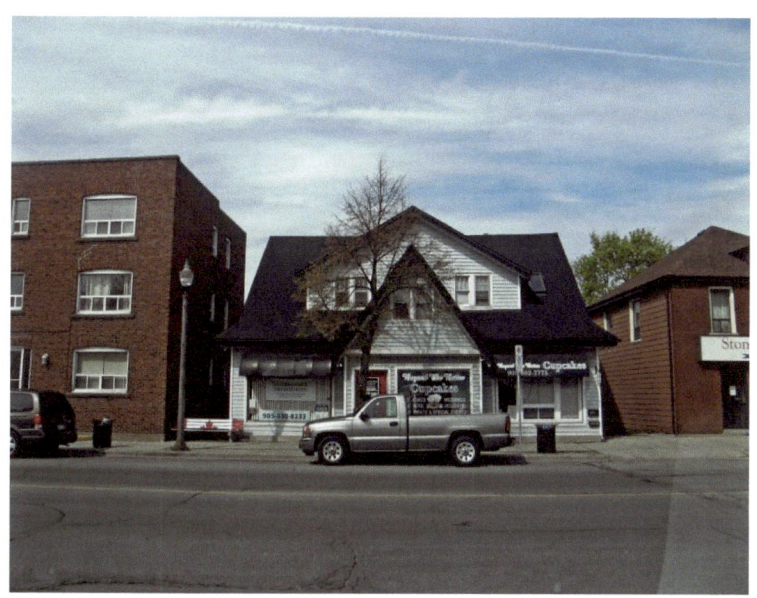

King Street

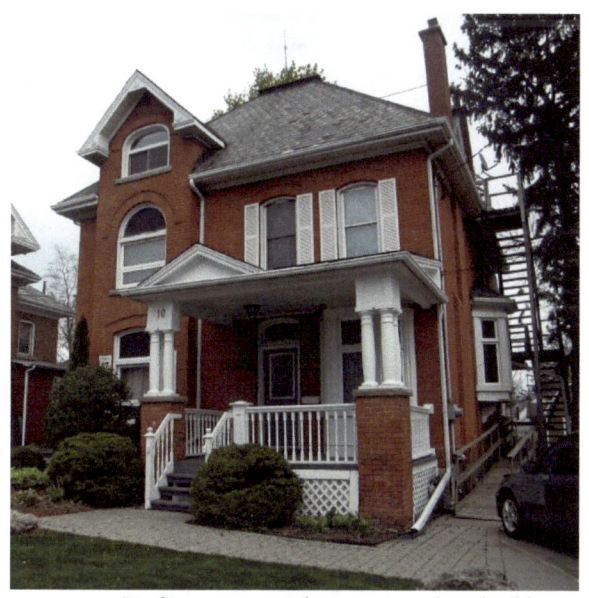

10 Lake Avenue – Italianate with two-and-a-half storey tower-
like bay with cornice return on gable,
pediment above verandah

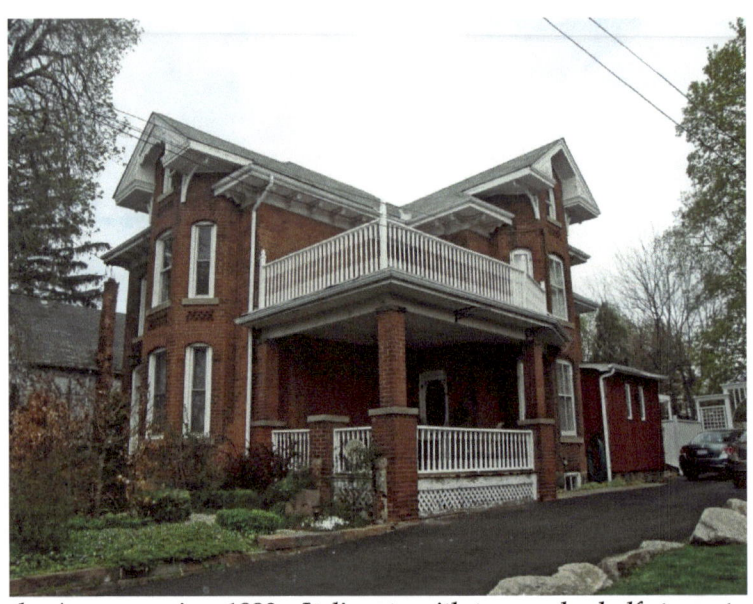

12 Lake Avenue – circa 1890 – Italianate with two-and-a-half storey tower-like bays with cornice return on gables,
cornice brackets, verandah on each storey
- Former Methodist Parsonage

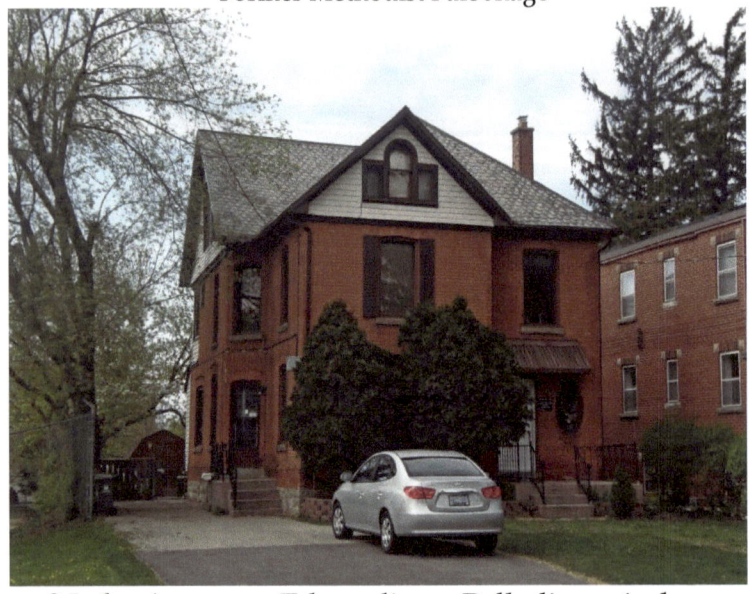

9 Lake Avenue – Edwardian – Palladian window

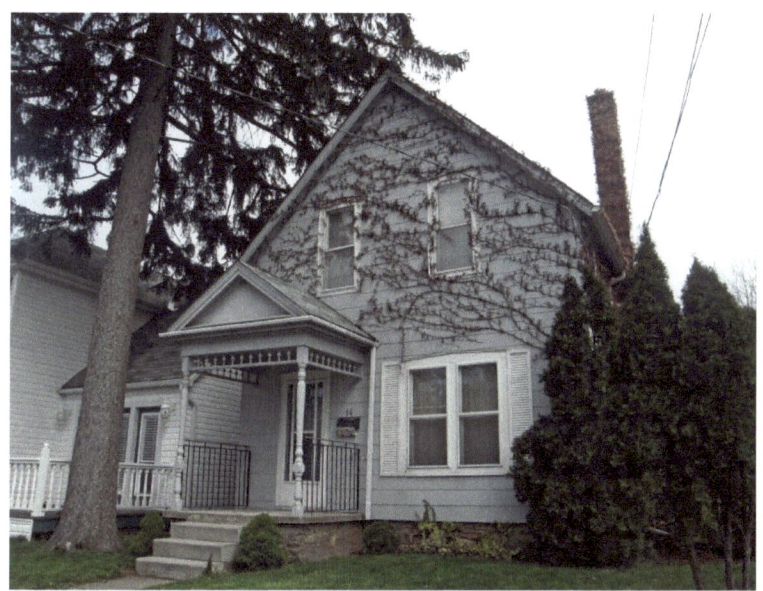

14 Lake Avenue – Gothic Revival, pediment above door

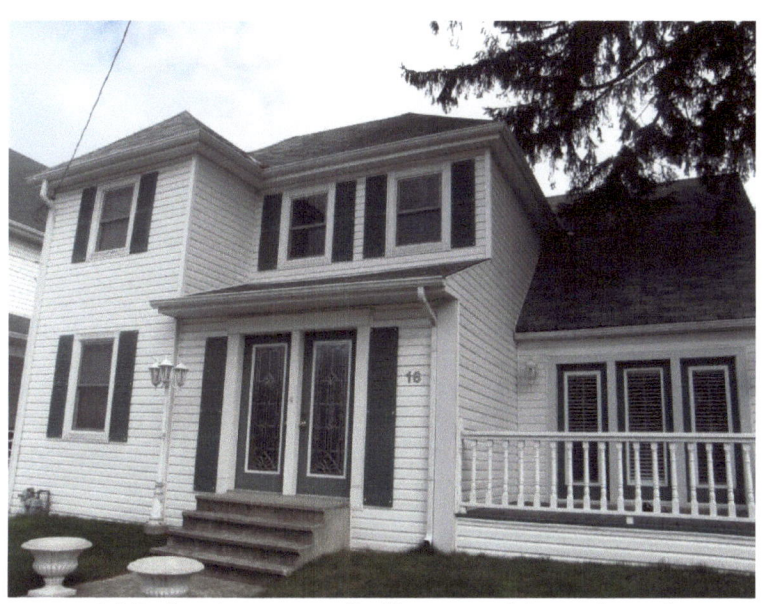

16 Lake Avenue – Italianate – hipped roof

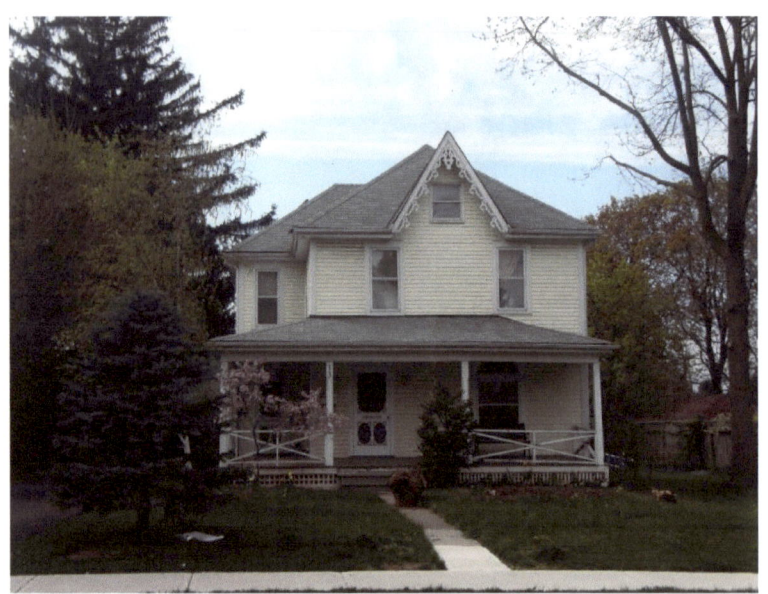

13 Lake Avenue – Gothic Revival,
vergeboard trim with finial on gable

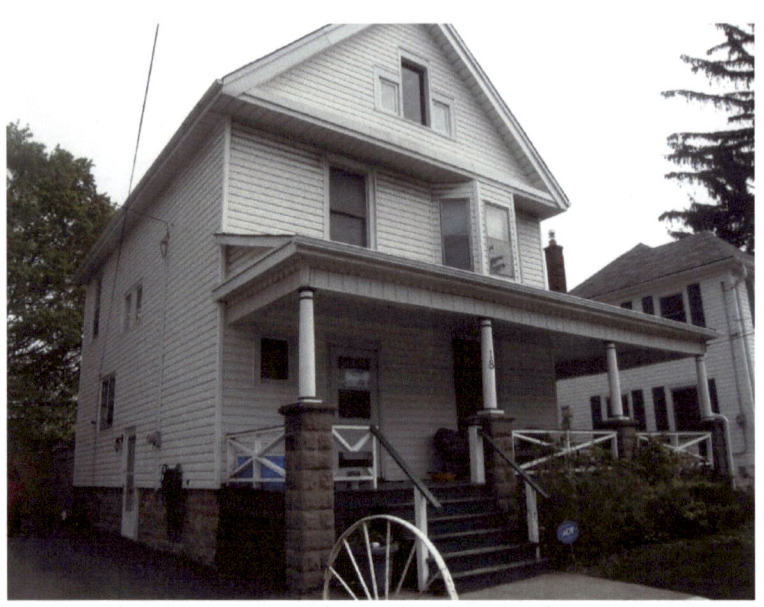

18 Lake Avenue – Edwardian, Palladian window

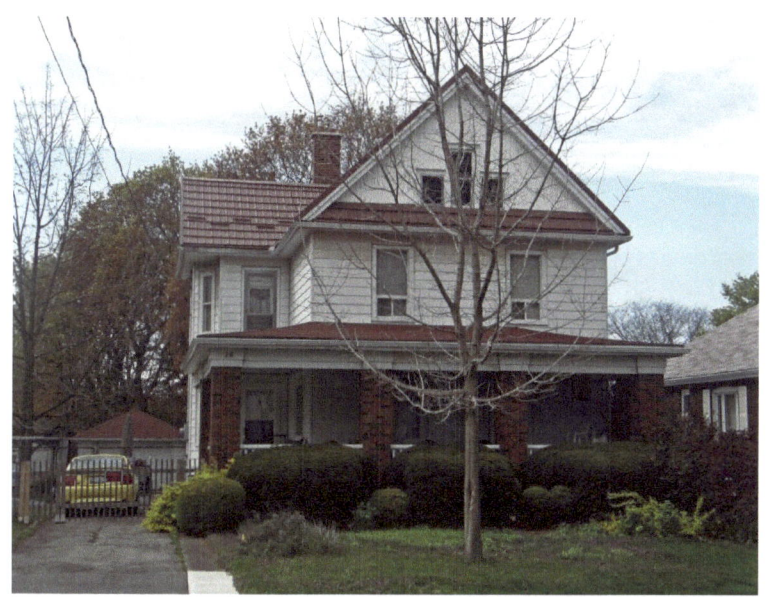

15 Lake Avenue – Edwardian, Palladian window

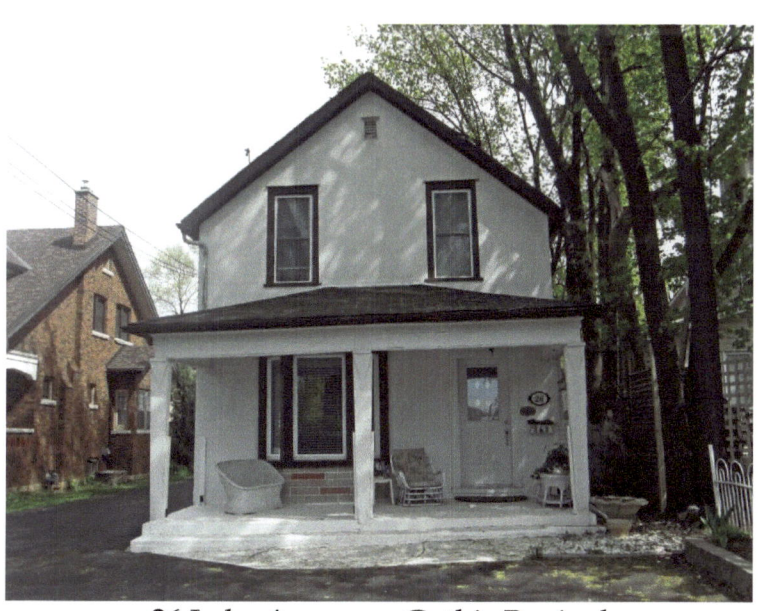

26 Lake Avenue – Gothic Revival

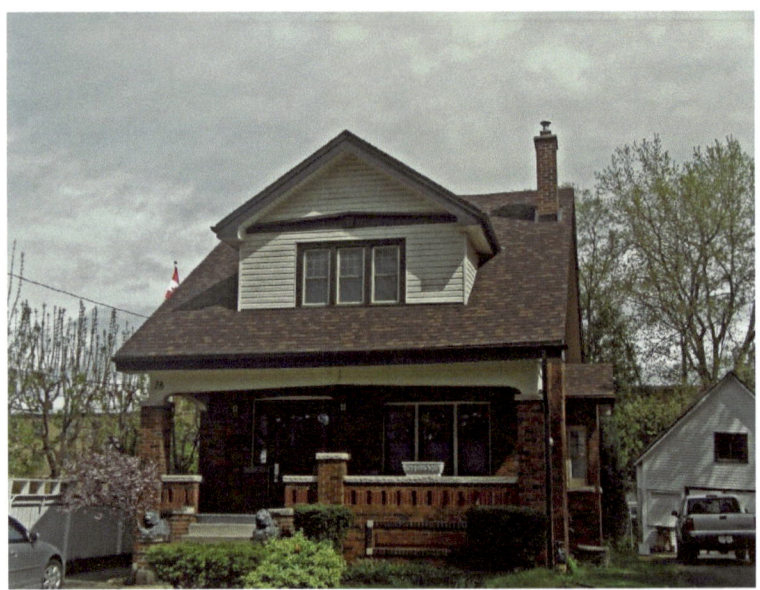

28 Lake Avenue – Gothic Revival, dormer in attic

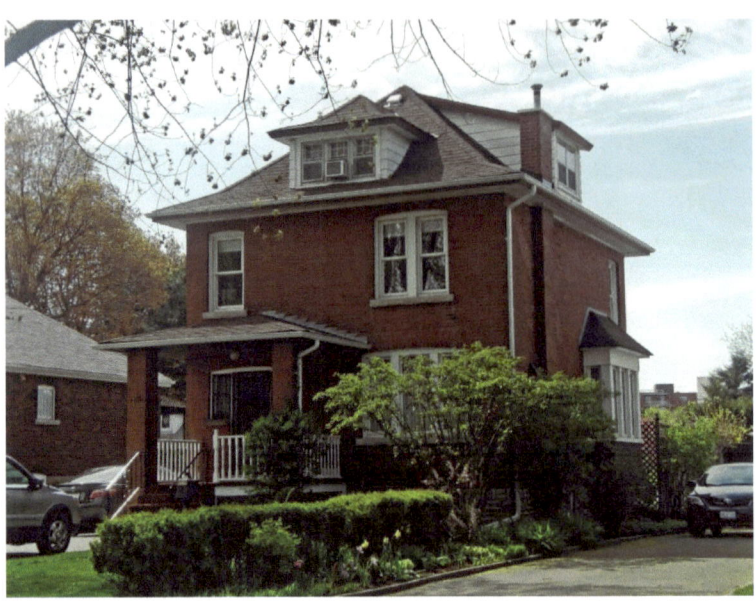

19 Lake Avenue – Italianate, dormers in attic

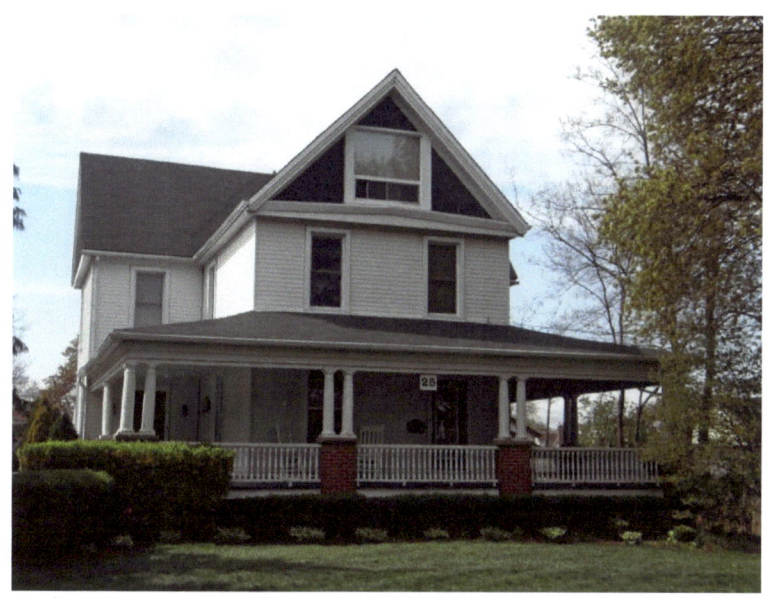

25 Lake Avenue – Edwardian style, wrap-around verandah

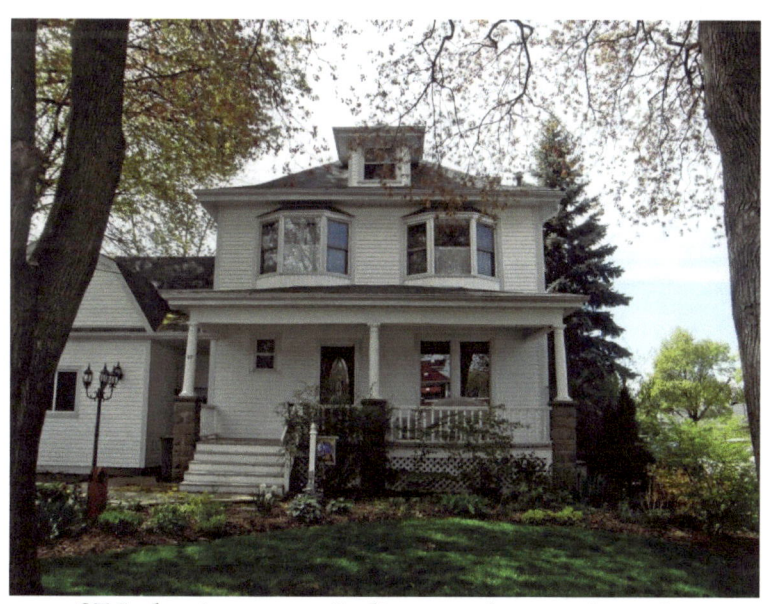

27 Lake Avenue – Italianate, dormer in attic,
bay windows on second storey

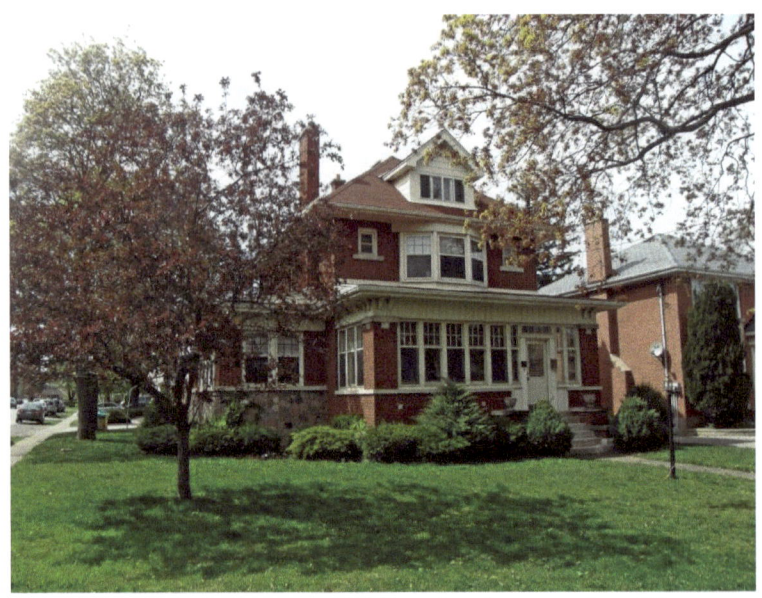

33 Lake Avenue – Italianate, dormer in attic,
bay window on second floor, enclosed sun porch

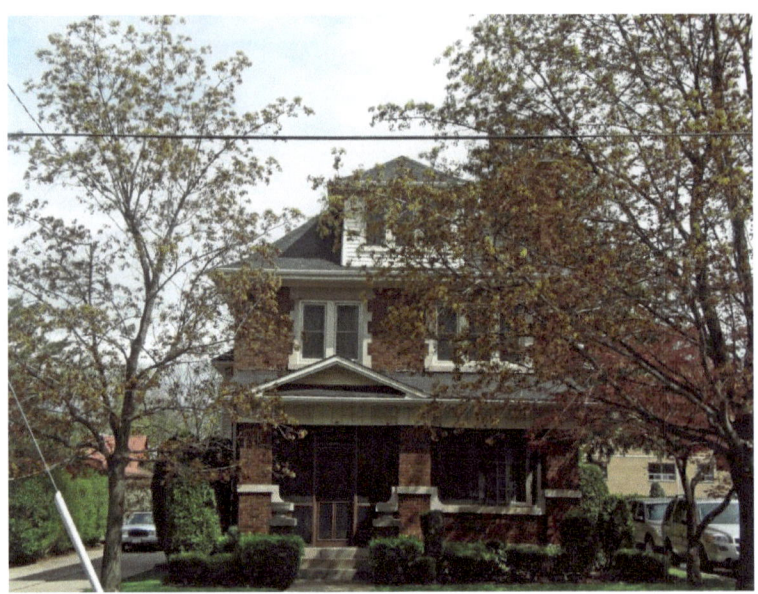

40 Lake Avenue – Italianate, dormer in attic

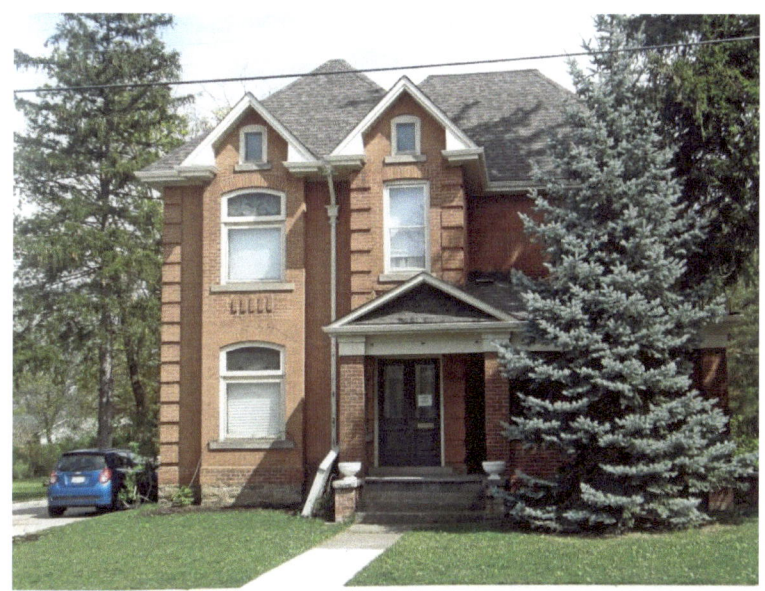

42 Lake Avenue – Roubos Greenhouses (garden plants) – Italianate with steeply pitched hip roof, two two-and-a-half storey tower-like bays with cornice return on gables, corner quoins, pediment above doorway

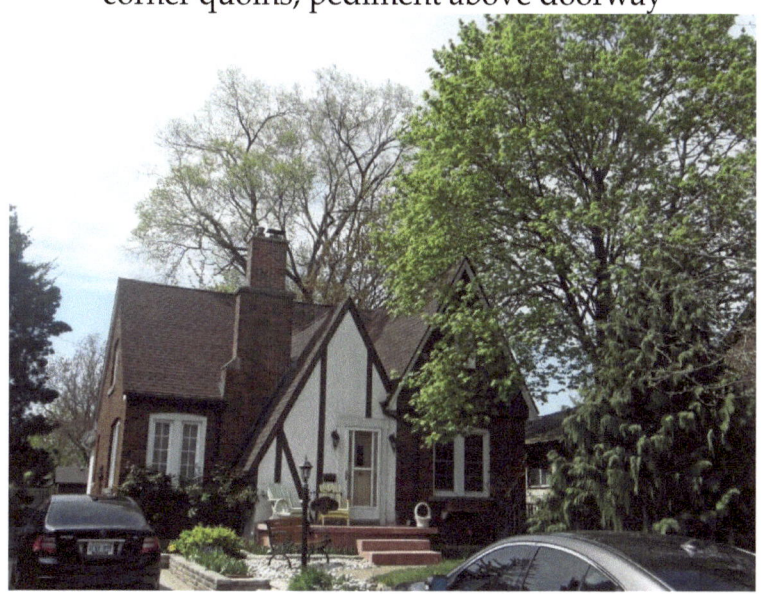

39 Lake Avenue

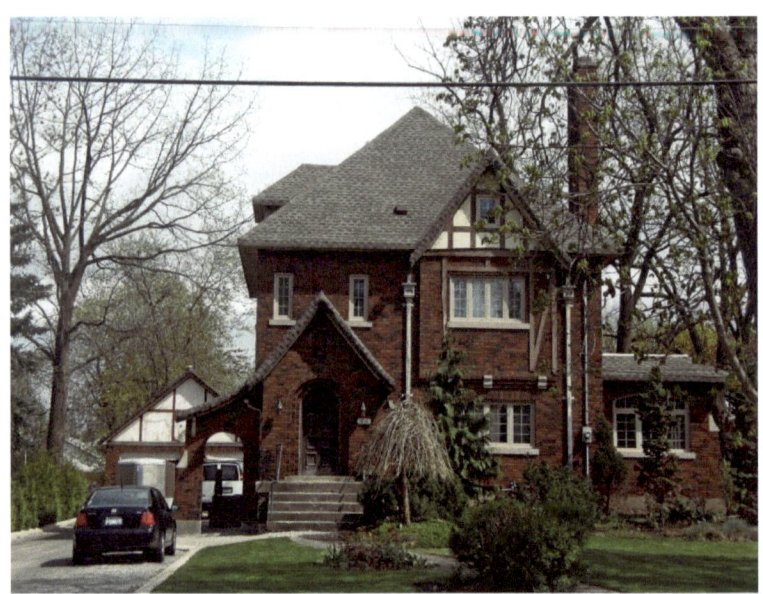

44 Lake Avenue – Tudor accents on gable

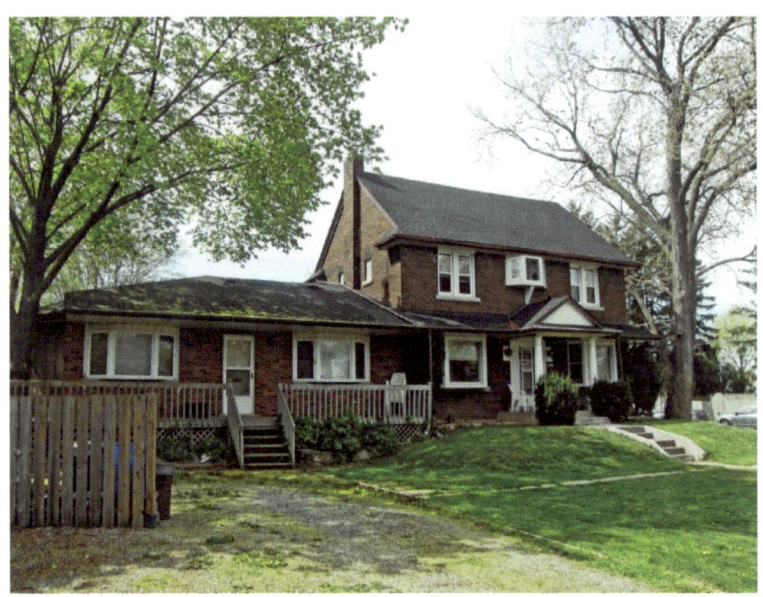

43 Lake Avenue – Gothic Revival, pediment above door

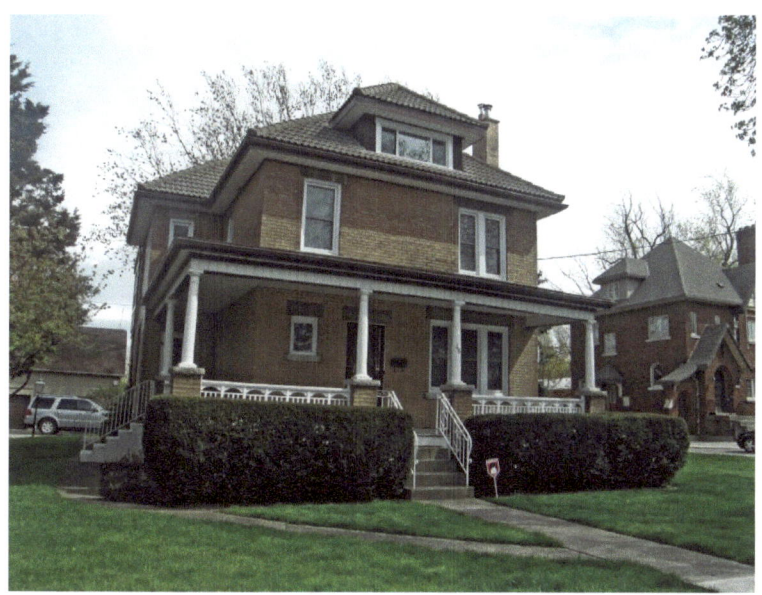

46 Lake Avenue – Italianate, hip roof, dormer in attic, Doric pillars

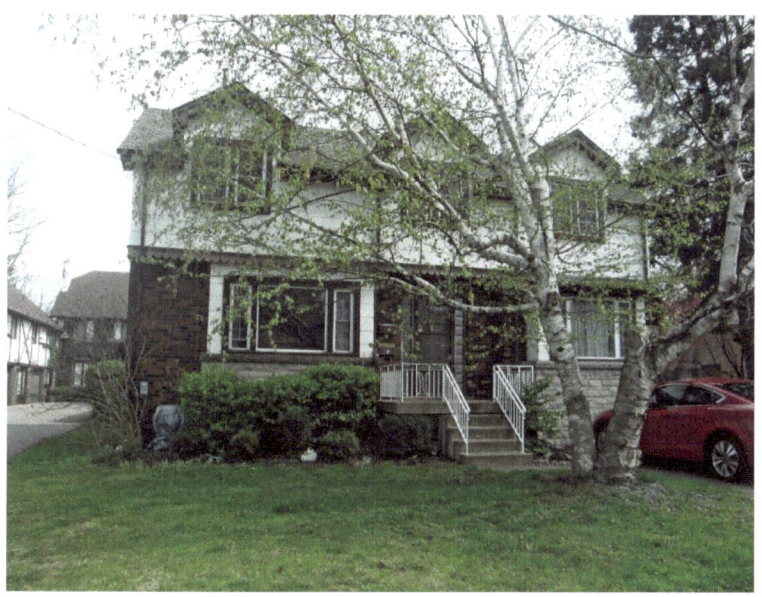

48 Lake Avenue

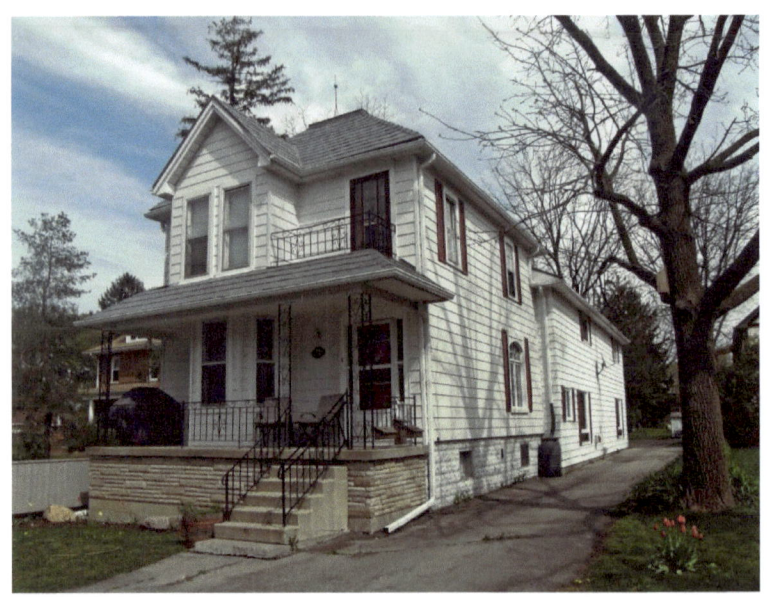

52 Lake Avenue – Italianate with two-storey frontispiece with gable, balcony on second floor

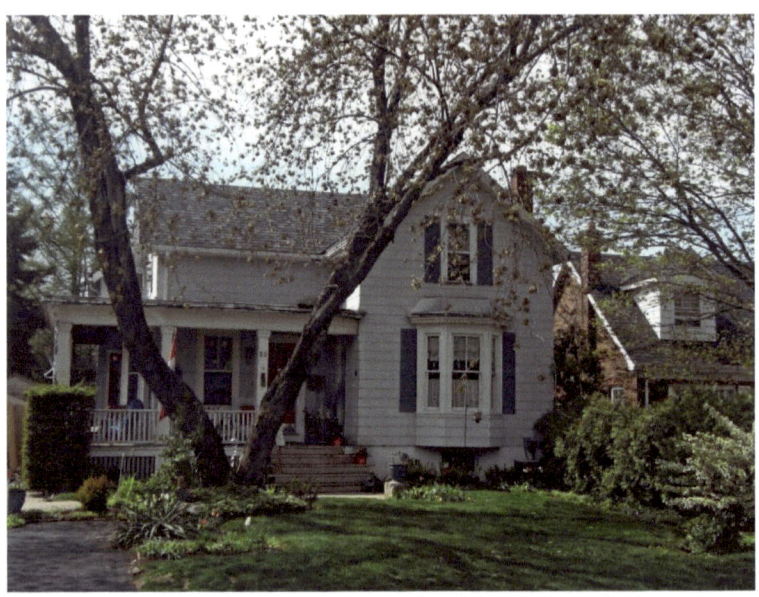

53 Lake Avenue – Gothic Revival

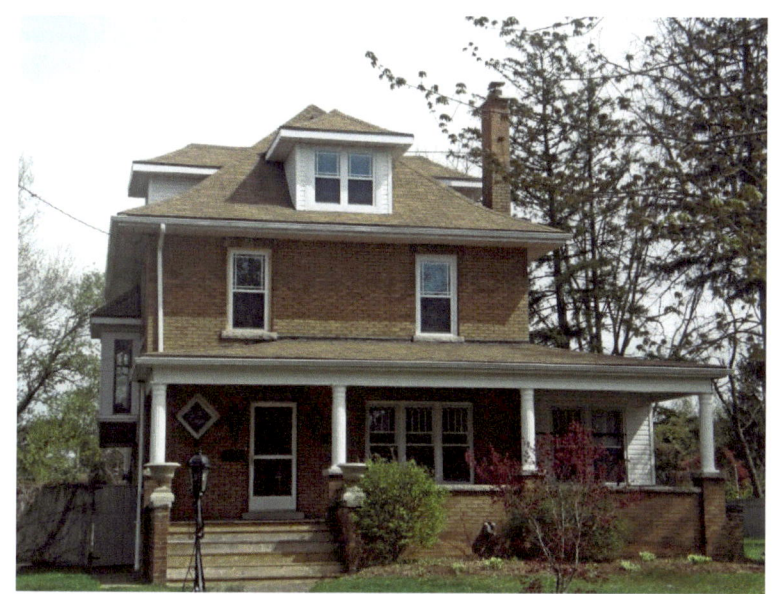

54 Lake Avenue – Italianate – dormer in attic, Doric pillars

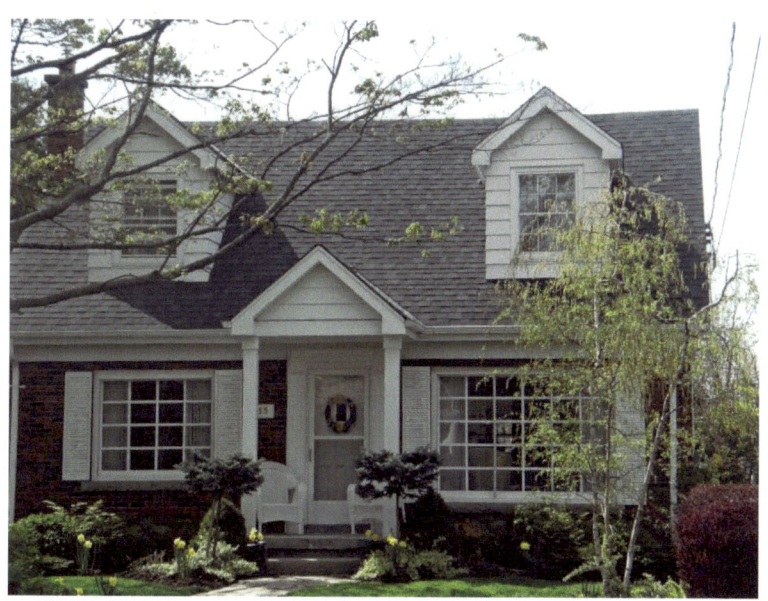

55 Lake Avenue – Gothic Revival, dormers in attic,
pediment above door

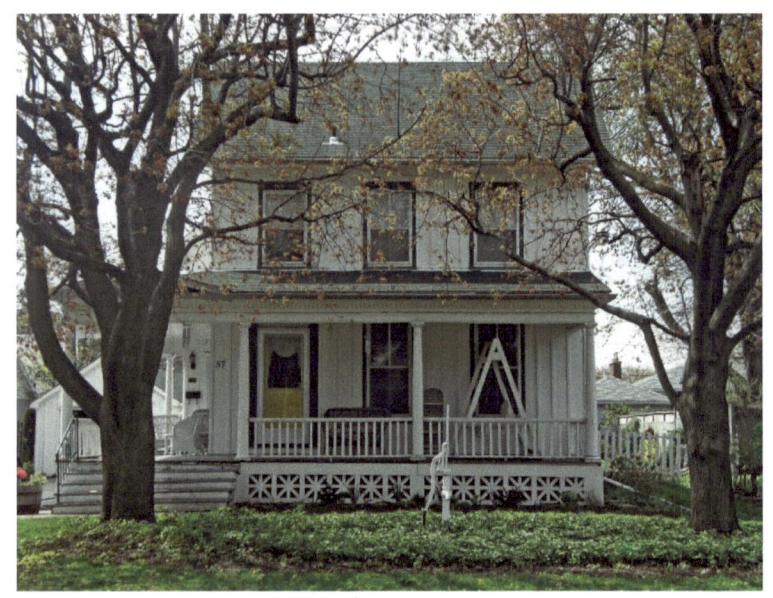

57 Lake Avenue

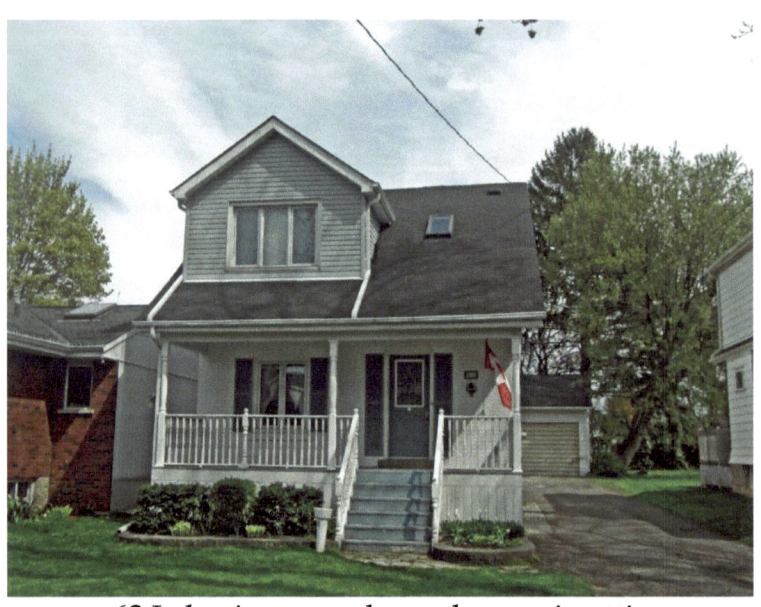

62 Lake Avenue – large dormer in attic

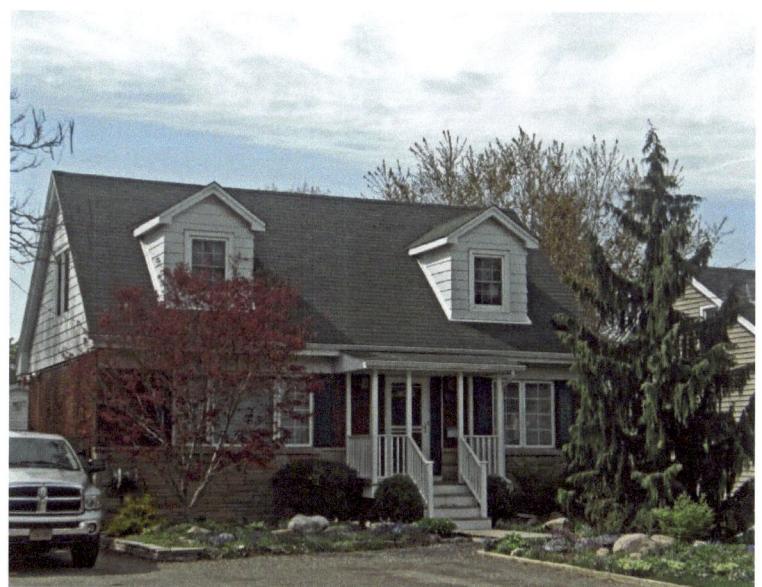

63 Lake Avenue – Gothic Revival – dormers in attic

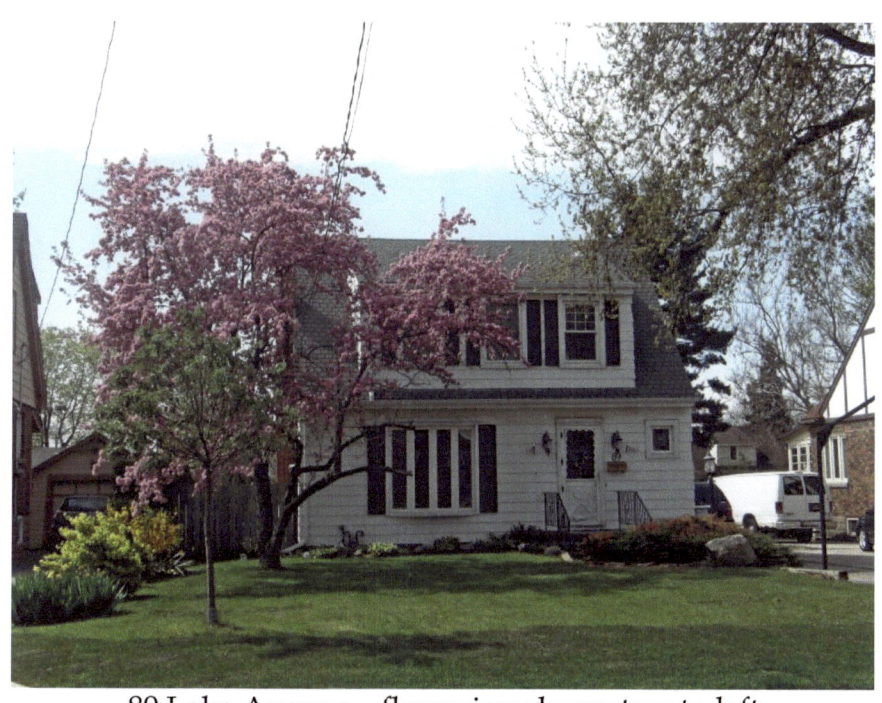

89 Lake Avenue – flowering cherry tree to left

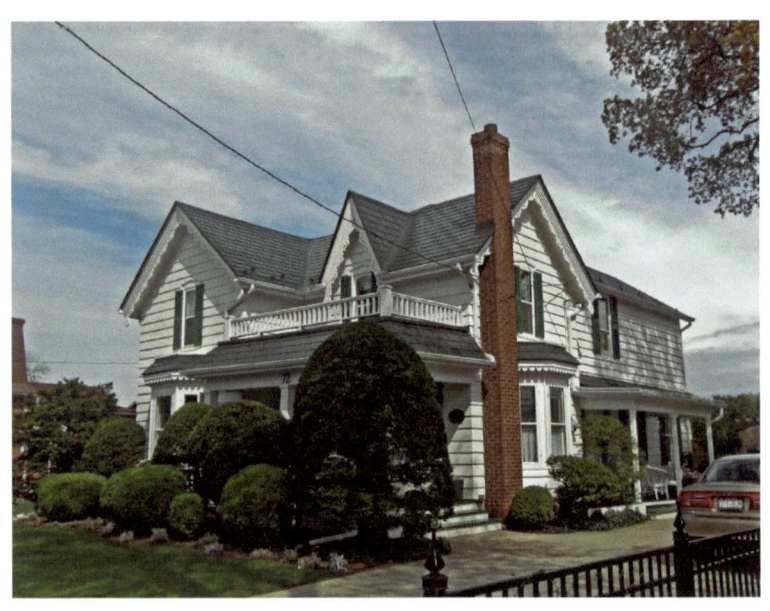

72 Lake Avenue – Gothic Revival - gingerbread trim

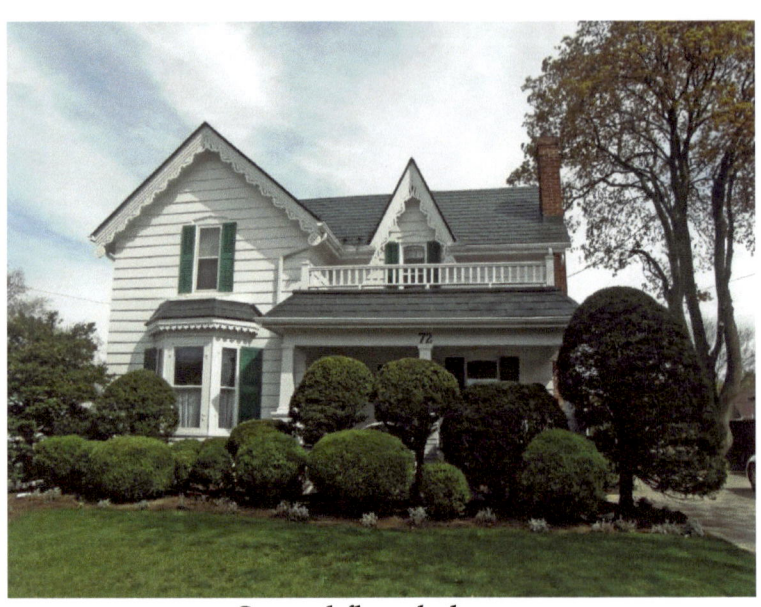

Second floor balcony

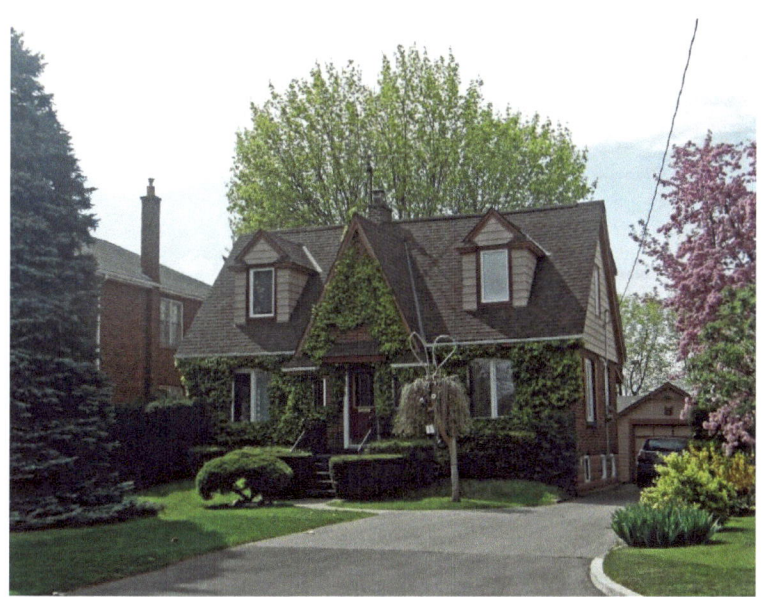

Gothic Revival – dormers in attic

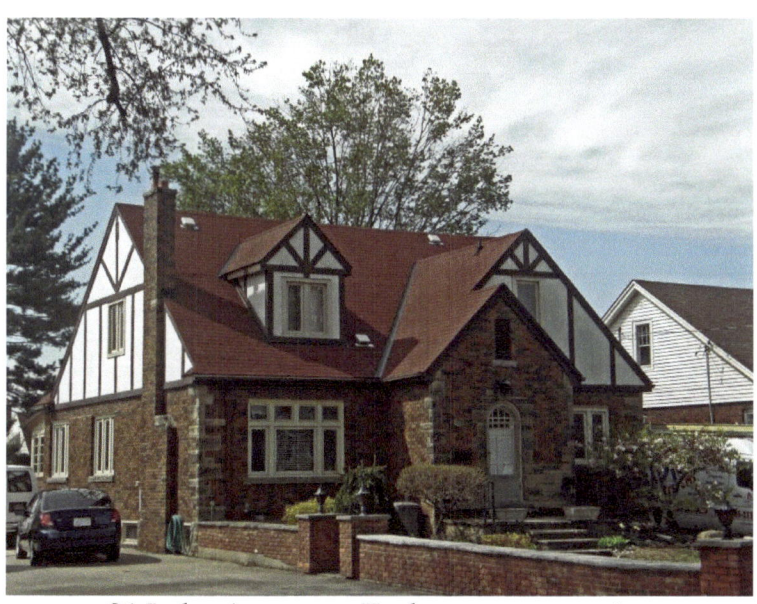

91 Lake Avenue – Tudor, corner quoins

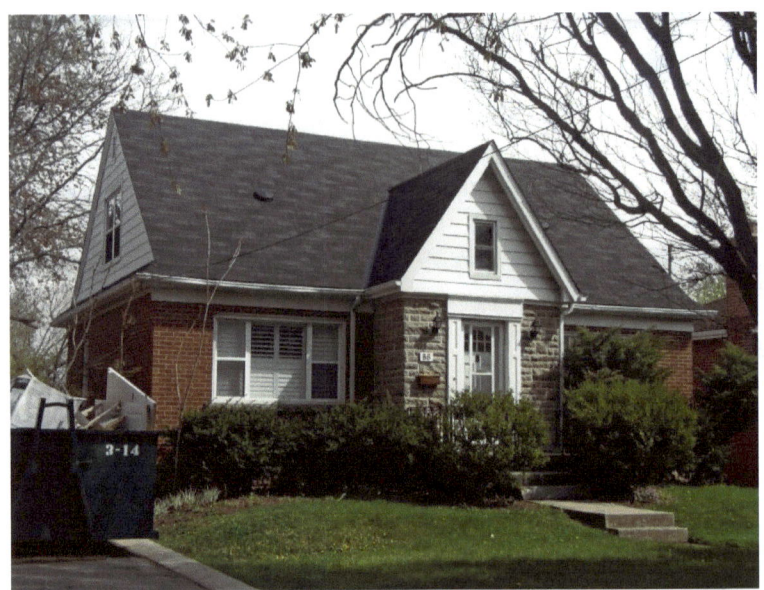

86 Lake Avenue – Gothic Revival

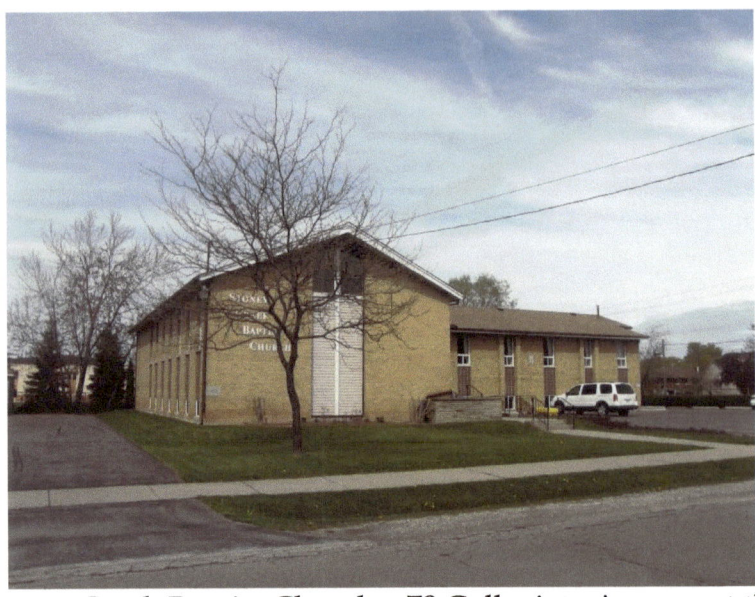

Stoney Creek Baptist Church – 79 Collegiate Avenue at the corner of Gray Road – built in 1958

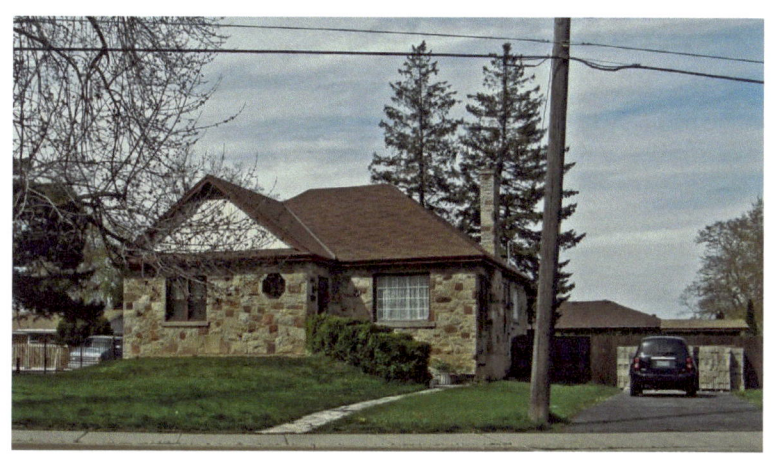

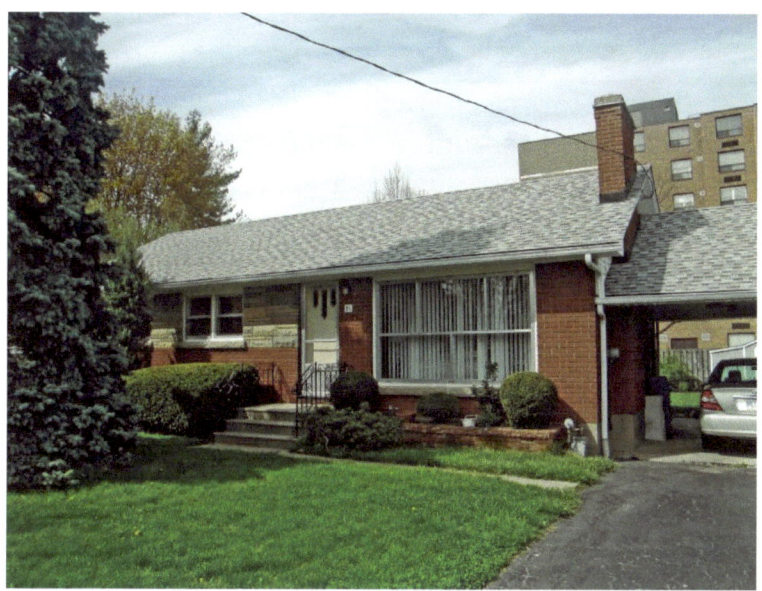

91 Donn Avenue – home of Harris and Denise Raue

Brackets: a decorative or weight-bearing structural element which forms a right angle with one side against a wall and the other under a projecting surface such as an eave or roof. Example: 12 Lake Avenue	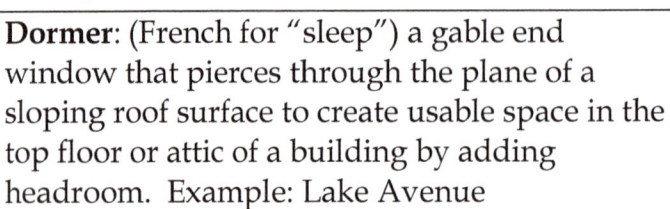
Cornice: originally the wooden overhang of the roof. With the use of stone, brick, iron and steel, the cornice is any projecting shelf at the top of a ceiling or roof. They can be very decorative. Example: 10 Lake Avenue	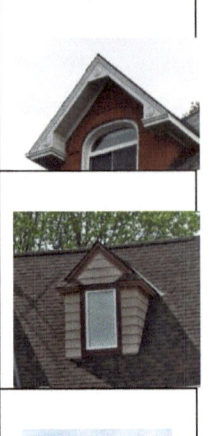
Cornice Return: decorative element on the end of a gable. Example: 10 Lake Avenue	
Dormer: (French for "sleep") a gable end window that pierces through the plane of a sloping roof surface to create usable space in the top floor or attic of a building by adding headroom. Example: Lake Avenue	
Finial: ornament added to the top of a gable, pinnacle, canopy or spire – a Gothic element. Example: 13 Lake Avenue	
Gable: the triangular portion of a wall between the edges of a sloping roof. Example: 72 Lake Avenue	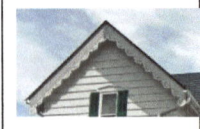

Hipped Roof: a roof where all sides slope downwards to the walls with no gables. Example: 26 King Street	
Palladian Window: a large window that is divided into three sections with the centre section larger than the two side sections and usually arched. Example: 16 Jones Street	
Pediment: a triangular section above the horizontal structure (entablature), typically supported by columns. The inside of the triangle is called the tympanum. Example: 42 Lake Avenue	
Quoin: masonry blocks at the corner of a wall, often a decorative feature, usually larger or of a different colour than the rest of the wall. Example: 42 Lake Avenue	
Vergeboards: also called bargeboards – hang from the projecting end of a roof and are often elaborately carved and ornamented. Example: 16 Jones Street	

Edwardian, 1900-1930 – This style bridges the ornate and elaborate styles of the Victorian era and the simplified styles of the 20th century. Balanced facades, simple roof lines, dormer windows, large front porches, and smooth brick surfaces are its characteristics. Example: 15 Lake Avenue	
Georgian, before 1860 – This style began with the British King Georges in the 18th century. These buildings have balanced facades around a central door, medium-pitched gable roofs, and small paned windows. Example: Nash-Jackson House	
Gothic Revival, 1830-1890 – These decorative buildings have sharply-pitched gables with highly detailed vergeboards, pointed-arch window openings, and dichromatic brickwork. It is a common style in Ontario. Example: 72 Lake Avenue	
Italianate, 1850-1900 – It has wide-bracketed eaves, belvederes, wrap-around verandahs.

Example: 19 Lake Avenue | |
| Tudor Revival – exposed timbers with stucco infill, multi-paned windows.

Example: 91 Lake Avenue | |

www.ingramcontent.com/pod-product-compliance
Lightning Source LLC
Chambersburg PA
CBHW041610180526
45159CB00002BC/799

* 9 7 8 1 5 0 0 4 6 2 6 6 6 *